A TALE OF
THREE TREES

A TALE OF THREE TREES

KEVIN J. CONNER

Published by Conner Ministries Ltd

CONNER
MINISTRIES

WEB: kevinconner.org
Email: kevin.conner321@gmail.com

Visit www.amazon.com/author/kevinjconner for a list of
other books by Kevin Conner.

Table of Contents

Introduction   **Page - 1-4**

One - The Tree of the Knowledge of Good and Evil
                                    Page- 5-17
  1. Back to the Beginning
  2. The One Commandment
  3. The Enemy - the Serpent
  4. The Why of the Tree of the Knowledge of Good and Evil
  5. Deceiving the Bride
  6. Seven Steps in the Fall
  7. The End Result
  8. That Tree is in us

Two - The Tree of Calvary   **Page - 18-29**
  1. The Purpose of Redemption is Restoration
  2. The Tree in the Book of Acts
  3. The Tree in the Book of Galatians
  4. The Tree in the Epistle of Peter
  5. The Tree in the Book of Exodus
  6. The Tree in the Book of Proverbs
  7. The Cross is a Tree
  8. Back to Faith and Obedience
     Summary - The Two Trees

Three - The Tree of Eternal Life   **Page -30-40**
  1. The Tree of Life in the Book of Revelation
  2. Making an End of Sin
     In Conclusion + Diagram to Illustrate

About the Author   43
Other Resources   44

A TALE OF THREE TREES

INTRODUCTION

One of the great hermeneutical principles of understanding and interpreting the Scriptures is the Symbolic Principle. The reader is referred to Bibliography and Chapter 19 in the textbook, "Interpreting the Scriptures" (Conner/Malmin - pages 140-145).

In brief, from this textbook, we note some major points. These things become the safe and Scriptural foundation for this booklet on "A Tale of Three Tress."

Though the word "symbol" is not specifically used in the Bible, God used the writers of Scripture to employ the literary method of symbolization in Scripture. They often used one thing to represent another because of common characteristics common to both.

God, in authoring Scripture, dealt with both creation and redemption. In Genesis chapters 1-2 we have the record of the creation of the natural realm: in the rest of Bible God uses the natural things He created to become symbols (Rom.1:19,20). In other words, the language of creation becomes the language of the symbol which is turns becomes the language of redemption,

Thus we have:
1. Symbolic objects - Hos.7:8; Psa.18:2; Prov.18:2; Psa.119:105; Rev.1:20
2. Symbolic Creatures - Dan.7:17; Hos.7:11; Lke.13:31,32; Isa.40:31; Jhn.1:29,36
3. Symbolic Numbers - 2Cor.13:1; Matt. 19:28; Gen.14:4

1

4. Symbolic Names - 1Sam.25:25; 4:21; Hos.1:9; Jhn.1:42
5. Symbolic Colours - Isa.1:18; Rev.3:4,5; 19:8
6. Symbolic Directions - Jer.1:14; 2Chron.4:4; Dan.8:4
7. Symbolic Places - Egypt, Canaan, the Wilderness, etc.

Some qualifications:
1. If the language of Scripture makes common sense, seek no other sense or it can become non-sense.
2. If it makes common or literal sense, then it can only be interpreted to have symbolic sense when the Scripture interprets this to be so (e.g., The Tabernacle, Jhn.1:14; The Temple, 1Cor.3:17).
3. The interpreter must recognize that the significance of a symbol is based upon the literal or actual nature and characteristics of that which is being used as a symbol. These characteristics must be drawn out from the literal or actual created thing or creature.
4. Sometimes there are both good and evil aspects of the created literal used in symbolic sense (e.g., the Serpent is used of both Satan and Christ - Rev.12:9; Jhn.3:14,15).

The main thing to keep in mind is that God uses the literal or actual things in symbolic sense. For the sake of repetition, the following columns illustrate he same truths.

Literal/Actual Creations	Used in Symbolic Sense
1.Sun, Moon, Stars-Gen.1	Woman's clothing -Rev.12
2.Fruit trees, seed, plants	Fruit of Spirit, Seed Word
3.Creation of Beasts/ Man	Man who becomes Beast
4.Light & Darkness divided	Kingdom-Light &Darkness
5.Waters above & seas	Wicked as troubled seas

And there are many, many examples in the Scriptures.

As mentioned, this becomes the foundation for this booklet on "A Tale of Three Trees. "

Now God has used a number of references to "Trees" that have both the literal/actual use and are yet used in symbolic sense. Following are a number of examples before launching into our study more fully as in this text.

1.The righteous are like a fruitful tree planted by the rivers of water that bring forth fruit in season. In contrast, the wicked are like the useless chaff (Psa. 1:3,4; Psa.92:12-15).

2. Israel becomes like a fruitless vine, fit only for the fire (Jer.2:21; Ezek.15)

3. The glory of King Nebuchadnezzar, King of Babylon, became like a cut down tree for seven years, and then restored under God (Dan.4)

4.The Kingdom of Heaven is like a mustard seed and in time becomes a great tree with birds in the branches and animals in its shadow (Matt.13:31,32)

5.Jesus likens Himself and His chosen disciples to a vine with branches bearing fruit (Jhn.15:1-16).

6.The true Israel of God, composed of believing Jews and Gentiles is likened to a faith olive tree also (Rom11:15-24).

7.Finally, there is the parable of the trees who went forth to find and anoint a King to rule over them. But none of them would leave their fruitfulness for position or power over the other trees (Jud.9).

Enough has been given to understand how **God uses trees** in symbolic sense as well as in literal or actual sense.

This booklet centres around three trees in Scripture:
1. The Tree of the Knowledge of Good and Evil
2. The Tree of Calvary
3. The Tree of Eternal Life

The Bible in Genesis opens with a Garden of Trees, and then these two important trees are brought to our attention. The whole history of the human race centres round these two trees. The Bible closes with but one tree, the Tree of Eternal Life.

We are not "spiritualizing" or "allegorizing" these trees. They undoubtedly were literal or actual trees, but they do have their spiritual and symbolic meanings also. When the title of this booklet says "**A Tale of Three Trees**", we are not doing away with the actuality of these trees. We are saying that these three trees also have symbolic sense behind and associated with them. This truth must be kept in mind throughout the study. There is the literal and symbolic sense interwoven through the study of the three trees.

When the word "Tale" is used, it is not referring to "Old wives' tales" (1Tim.4:7). Or "Fairy Tales", which generally are not true or factual. Collin's Dictionary speaks of "A Tale" as being , "A narrative, a story; that which is told and reported; disclosure of something secret." This is the true story of the Bible, the entrance of sin, the Fall of Mankind by eating of the forbidden Tree and through Calvary's Tree, the restoration through redemption of the Tree of Eternal Life.
We can now proceed to Chapter One.

CHAPTER ONE

THE TREE OF THE KNOWLEDGE OF GOOD and EVIL

1. Back to the Beginning

When God created mankind, Adam and his sinless and perfect bride, Eve, they were placed in a Garden of beautiful trees. The trees were pleasant to the eyes, and good for food. All were available to the man and the woman. They were the masters of created things. They were as king and queen together, made in the image and likeness of God (Gen.1:26-28; Gen.2).

2. The One Commandment

But there were two special trees in this earthly Paradise. They were named specifically "the tree of the knowledge of good and evil" and "the tree of life" (Gen.2:8,9; 3:22-24). Adam and his wife were not forbidden to eat of the Tree of Eternal Life. There was only ONE forbidden tree. There was only the one "you shall not…" There was only one law-word; one forbidden tree and all that it symbolized. That tree was the "Tree of the knowledge of good and evil."

The record runs like this. "And the Lord God took the man and put him in the Garden of Eden to dress it and to keep it. And the Lord commanded the man, saying, Of every tree of the garden, you may freely eat: But of the Tree of the Knowledge of Good and Evil, you shall not eat of it, for in the day you eat thereof, you shall surely die" (Gen.2:9, 15-17).

But, because of human nature, we sometimes - many times - skip over words and miss what it says and what the verse does not say. We see a sign "Wet Paint - Do not touch." But there is something in all of all that wants to and does 'touch the paint!'

These several verses illustrate. They are examples to us.

- It does not say only "the Tree of Knowledge."
- It does not say "The Tree of the Knowledge of Evil."
- But it says, "The Tree of the Knowledge of GOOD and EVIL." In other words, it was a mixture of both good AND evil.
- This was the one commandment. They were not to eat of this forbidden tree. They were not to violate this commandment to gain this type of dual knowledge.
- The penalty for eating of this forbidden tree was clearly spelt out. "In the day you eat thereof, you shall surely die." It may be safely said, "In the day you eat thereof, you shall surely die. Or, in dying (spiritually, you shall surely die (physically). It can be said, that, Adam died spiritually (separation from God and the life of God) in the 24-hour-day he sinned. But he died physically some 930 years later in "God's day" (Read 2Pet.3:8 with Psa.90:4). That is, even though the Patriarchs lived for years, no man ever lived "a day" (that is, God's day!).
- If Adam and his wife had not sinned by disobeying God's command, they could have lived "happily ever after." They would still be alive today, as the Tree of Eternal Life was not forbidden them.
- After God gave this commandment to Adam, He then formed or built a bride for Adam and we have the first marriage of one man and one woman (Gen.2:18-25).This may explain why the serpent came to the woman first. It should be remembered that the command was given to the man, Adam, before his bride was fashioned and brought to him!

3. The Enemy - The Serpent - Gen.3:1-6

BUT there was an enemy in the Garden, that earthly Paradise. We remember that God created the beasts of the field and Adam named them all (Gen.1:24,25; Gen.2:18-21; 3:1).

But here the literal or the actual becomes symbolic of that which is spiritual, The serpent, in time, is spoken of as "that old serpent, called the Devil and Satan" (Rev.12:9). He is the Dragon, the Accuser and he has many fallen angels with him (Rev.12:7-10). Once again, we see interwoven that which is the literal/actual and the symbolical, and the spiritual.

Debate rises often whether it was a literal or actual snake (serpent) or trees, but we need to keep in mind the principle of 1Cor.10:1-4 as we interpret various passages of Scripture.

Within and interwoven is the literal/actual and the spiritual/symbolical. This is seen woven throughout the Word. In this passage of Corinthians, Paul is not allegorizing or spiritualizing away the miracles in any way.

There is the actual miracle of the smitten Rock, and the flowing of the waters literally and actually. Paul is showing that within or interwoven was both the literal/actual and the spiritual and symbolical. Balance is important in handling the Scriptures pertaining to these things.

BUT, returning from this diversion, we see in Genesis that there was an enemy - that OLD serpent, the Devil and Satan.

He hates God. He hated the man and the woman God had created. He would do in earth what he did in heaven. That is. Bring about the Fall of the man and the woman God created in His image. Man was made a little lower than the angels (Psa.8 with Heb.2). Man was given a mandate: Be fruitful, multiply, reproduce, have dominion over the earth, rule over creation as king and queen under God.

Satan, the serpent, hates this, as it were a new creation of beings, this new order of beings.

But there is only one way he can bring about this Fall. It was Satan's three-pronged attack. It was his evil purpose:
- Attack the law-word or the commandment God gave them.
- Undermine their faith in God and His word.
- Get them to disobey God and get them off of the ground of faith and obedience on to the ground of unbelief and disobedience.
(Refer to Diagram which illustrates these things).

4. **The 'Why' of the Tree of Knowledge of Good and Evil?**
One may ask, WHY did God put that Tree of the Knowledge of Good and Evil in the Garden? Why, when God knew if man partook of this tree - and God knew he would - there would follow the tragic history of the human race. Isn't like the sign "Wet Paint - Do not touch" being put there? Human nature is to touch it! But the Serpent, Satan, will encourage them to take the forbidden fruit. This will be seen in our study.

The reason God put this tree there was twofold:
- It was a test of FAITH in His person; who He was
- It was a test of OBEDIENCE to His spoken Word.

Faith and obedience! They would have to trust God and His word, that there was a Divine reason why God did not want them to eat of the forbidden tree and out of that trust would come obedience to God's and His word.

The old Gospel Song says it well:

"Trust and obey; for there's no other way,

To be happy in Jesus, but to trust and obey."

5. Deceiving the Bride, Eve - 1Tim.2:4; 2Cor.11:2,3

Paul expresses his concern and fear for the Corinthian believers that, what happened to Eve would happen to the Church.

Eve is a type of the Church, the Bride of Christ (Eph.5:22-33). Adam is a type of Christ when in his sinless state.

Paul says: "As Eve was corrupted in her mind" or "deceived..." Eve was deceived, beguiled by the serpent, deceived in her mind.

It may be asked: Why did the serpent come to Eve, to the woman, to Adam's beautiful bride? On a surface reading of Gen.3:6b, it looks as if Adam was standing right there with Eve when she partook of the forbidden tree, However, the Scriptures, both in Corinthians and Timothy would imply that she was on her own, or by herself alone. And again, it is hard to believe that Adam would just be standing there, allowing his wife to be challenged over the law-word of God and thus open to deception. What kind of a husband would he be? It should be remembered that God gave the commandment to Adam, THEN created the bride for Adam after His command to Adam. He must have passed that law-word on to his wife after the marriage.

9

Note also 1Cor.1:10. "For this cause ought the woman to have (a covering, or authority) power on her head because of the angels."

The NKJV puts it this way. "For this reason the woman ought to have a symbol of authority on her head because of the angels" (Read also 1Cor.11:1-16).

Remember that the serpent is Satan, a fallen angel, and he comes to the woman to tempt her to disobey God's commandment. Here, the woman, Eve, is away from her "covering", her husband Adam. The serpent, the fallen angel, Lucifer or Satan, comes to tempt her. The commandment had been specifically given to Adam and no doubt he passed it on to his wife, Eve. And so the serpent comes to deceive the bride. Paul in Timothy is clear. Adam was not deceived but the woman, being in the transgression, was deceived (1Tim.1:13,14).

6. Seven Steps in the Fall

We consider the attack on the law-word, their faith in that word, and their joint-disobedience to that word.

(i)   The Serpent puts a doubt into Eve's mind over the law-word. "Has God said?"

This is Satan's first utterance recorded in the Bible. It is an attack on the word of God - what God said (Gen.2:16,17). His will is His word, and His word is His will. It was an attack on God's law by the lawless one, the one commandment under which God placed man.

"Sin is transgression of the law" - 1Jhn.3:14. To break the one commandment was really to break them all (Jas.1:10). It was a doubt on the authority of the spoken word of God. The

10

old saying is true. Doubt is the father of the lie! It was the seed of unbelief; a doubt on the word. It was the seed of doubt.

The serpent's tactics are the same today. He puts a question mark over the spoken and the written Word of God in the minds and hearts of people. "Who wrote the Bible?" So many mistakes, contradictions, translations? Is it inspired, infallible? Doubt is placed over the plenary-verbal inspiration of the Scriptures, the thoughts and words inspired by God.

The seed of sin entered the mind (2Cor.11:2,3).

What should Eve have done? She should have ran to her husband, Adam, and tell him "there was an occult meeting going on in the garden by this snake in the grass!" The Devil is the same throughout the ages and still puts the doubt in the mind of people over the law-word of God. He has not changed!

(ii)   The Woman, Eve, adds to the law-word of God.

"You must not eat of it or touch it; if you do you will die." There is no specific word that says exactly that. Eve should not have entered into the conversation with the serpent. There was nothing to discuss, God had said it. That settles it. There was nothing to discuss with the serpent, who was the Devil. Eve should have gone to Adam and let him settle it. But the doubt was in her mind.

(iii)   The Woman, Eve, adulterates or waters the law-word down.

How? She should have stopped any further discussion with the serpent. But she said,

11

"LEST we die..." (Gen.3:3). God had said "You shall surely die" or "most certainly die (Gen.2:16,17). The word "lest" means "in case we die." (Read also Jhn.5:14).

This word took away the full meaning of what God had actually said, when He said "You shall SURELY die" as the next step shows. Eve watered the word down, taking away its full effect.

(iv)   The Serpent lied outright against the law-word.

This is the second utterance of Satan in the Scripture. It is an outright lie. He is a liar and the father of it. "When he speaks a lie, he speaks from his own resources, for he is a liar and the father of it" (Jhn.8:44,45. NKJV).

The first utterance was a doubt.

The second utterance was a lie.

The doubt is indeed father to the lie!

Read 2Thess.2:7-12. Paul writes about "believing the lie" or "believing the truth." He encourages the Thessalonians to have a LOVE for the truth. All will believe one or the other. There is no neutral ground.

God had said: "You shall surely die."

Satan said: "You shall NOT surely die."

One was the truth of God. One was the lie of Satan. Which would Eve believe? The truth of God or the lie of Satan? The lie speaks exactly opposite to the truth,

The entire world believes one way or the other. There is still the attack on the word of God, People, if they do not have a love for the truth, receive a strong delusion and believe a lie. People will disbelieve what Satan does

12

believe (Satan believes in heaven, hell, sin and death). He gets people to disbelieve what he does believe! The only way out of deception is to have a LOVE for the truth, even if it hurts. Know the truth and it (He) will set you free (Jhn.8:33-36).

(v)   The Serpent Slanders the law-word of God.
It is important to understand the word "slander" as used here. Charles Finney defines the word as "to tell the truth in such a way as to give the lying impression."

We note the use of the word in the following Scriptures   (Num.14:36;   Prov.10:18; Psa.31:13;   1Tim.3:11).   The   12   spies slandered the Promised Land. They said "it is a good land, BUT the giants are there."

How did the serpent slander to the woman about this tree? He said: "God knows that in the day you eat thereof, you will be as gods, knowing good and evil."

There was part truth here. God does know good and evil but can only and eternally be good and do good (Read carefully Gen.3:22-24).

There was part lie here also. Man would come to know good and evil and could only do evil apart from God's prevenient or restraining grace.

The slander? God knows something you do not know. There is something in that Tree of the Knowledge of Good and Evil that God does not want to you to know and have. Why is that?

Satan attacks God intentions, God's motives. The serpent suggests that they are evil

13

motives. Why can't you eat of that tree? God is withholding that privilege from you. You really are not a free-will creature. You are slaves to someone else's will. Thus slandering God's holy nature. Telling the truth in such a way as to give the false or the lying impression! That's it!

(**Note:** It is possible that God wanted man to have this knowledge of good and evil, BUT not by way of tragic experience! It is the same generally for parents and their children. They want them to know the tragic effects of evil drugs BUT NOT BY WAY OF EXPERIENCE!)

Human history and human experience has proved the tragic results of eating of the forbidden tree. This is by extremely sad and tragic experience! And we all know that!)

(vi) The Woman, Eve, is deceived by the Serpent's words - 1Tim.2:14; 2Cor.11:2,3.

"The woman was deceived…"

"The woman was beguiled…"

Eve turns from the word of God to the serpent's word. She believes the lie of Satan against the truth of God. There was the inward fall before the outward and external act of disobedience. It was the fall from faith in God's word.

Satan first and last weapon is deception (Rev.12). That old serpent that deceives the whole world.

"Faith comes by hearing and hearing by the Word (Rhema) of God" (Rom.10:17). Also, "Unbelief comes from hearing and hearing by the word of Satan."

14

The root sin was UNBELIF. The Holy Spirit comes to convict the world of sin "BECAUSE they believe not on Me..." (Jhn.16:7-11). Adam and Eve fell from faith to unbelief. They came on to the wrong ground. All the SINS of the world come from that ROOT SIN - UNBELIEF! Unbelief is the root sin. Jesus died for all sins, but the root sin of unbelief will send people to hell, a lost eternity. Sin is the root and sins are the fruit of that root sin - unbelief!

(vii) <u>The man and his wife, Adam and Eve, both disobey the commandment of the Lord.</u>

" ...she took of the fruit thereof and did eat, and gave also to her husband with her, and he did eat" (Gen.3:6).

The woman ate first, then the man. But the woman and the man both disobey the law-word of God. "Sin is transgression of the law" (1Jhn.3:14).

"Whatsoever is not of faith is sin" (Rom.14:23b).

"By one man's disobedience, many were made (constituted) sinners..." (Rom.5:19).

It may be asked: "Who was the worst sinner?" The Scripture provides the answer.

(i)   Eve was deceived or beguiled by the serpent.

(ii)   Adam was not deceived but sinned knowingly. Paul says: "By ONE MAN sin entered the world..." (Rom.5:12-21). The unborn human race was as yet in his loins, Adam

15

representing the whole race. It is "in Adam all die..." (1Cor.15:21,22).

(iii)   BOTH the woman and the man sinned. Both fell from grace. Both disobeyed the law-word. Both became evil. The woman was deceived, but the race was in Adam and brought evil on us all. Both need a redeemer!

7. The End Result?

The serpent, Satan, has accomplished what he set out to accomplish. He has gotten the first sinless bridegroom and bride off of the ground of faith and obedience over on to the ground of unbelief and disobedience. How? By attacking the law-word, the one commandment, that God gave to Adam and Eve. He attacked the Word of God. He took them from the Tree of Eternal Life that was available to them, and took them over to the Tree of the Knowledge of Good and Evil. We forfeited the best tree in Adam.

And so we are told that God drove the man and the woman out of the Garden of Eden (evidently they were reluctant to go). He placed at the gate of the Garden Cherubim and a flaming sword to guard the way to the Tree of Eternal Life (Gen.3:22-24). And the rest is the sad and tragic history of the human race!

Man needs a Redeemer from sin and unbelief. He needs someone to restore him back to the Garden of Paradise and open the way back to the Tree of Eternal Life.

8. That Tree in in us!

Before proceeding to the next chapter - the Tree of Calvary - we need to see that "The Tree of the Knowledge of Good and Evil" has found its roots in us. This is the battle ground; the ground of spiritual warfare, for the root or the law of sin has not yet been eradicated from us, regardless of what believer's hold doctrinally.

But this is what this section is about!

CHAPTER TWO

THE TREE OF CALVARY

1. The Purpose of Redemption is Restoration

With the fall if man, God was not caught unawares. He foreknew it. He foresaw it. He was prepared for it. God's plan of redemption came into operation immediately, and this upon Adam and Eve's response.

The purpose of God in redemption was restoration, the restoration of man back to the image of God, and back to the forfeited Tree of Eternal Life. Man sinned by a Tree, the Tree of the Knowledge of Good and Evil. Man forfeited the Tree of Eternal Life. Restoration by redemption would come about in due time by a Tree. That would be the Tree of Calvary.

However, in the meantime, God would introduce animal sacrifices before Jesus would die on the Tree of Calvary as the supreme and perfect sacrifice for sin.

- Adam and eve sinned by the Tree.
- A guilty conscience drove the man and his wife to make coverings for themselves to make themselves presentable and acceptable to God. This is seen in the fig leaves to cover their nakedness.
- God in grace comes seeking the man and his wife. Remember that grace is not man coming to God. It is God coming to man. It was God seeking man, not man seeking God.
- After a kind of "guilt and blame game" of Adam, Eve, and the Serpent, God killed a sinless, guiltless and

innocent animal to provide a covering for their nakedness. All shadowed forth the redemption in due time by Jesus Himself.

- The very fact that Adam and Eve accepted the coats of skin provided by the death of an innocent victim (the truth of substitution introduced here) show that, by faith, they accepted God's provided atonement.
- They could have maintained their fig-leaf covering (works of self-effort), but they accepted God's provided coats of skin and this by faith.
- Thus they were saved by faith in the body and blood of a substitutionary sacrifice.
- However, the death penalty was still in vogue. "In the day you eat thereof, in dying (spiritually) you will die (physically. So Adam died in the 24 hour-day he sinned, but died physically 930 years later.
- The Cherubim guarded the way to the Tree of Eternal Life until God's appointed time, as the 'Tabernacle' of that period of time.

God wanted to get mankind off of the ground of unbelief and disobedience back to the ground of faith and obedience. It is His desire to restore through redemption all that was forfeited in the Tree of Eternal Life. But the Redeemer must die on a "Tree", for the man sinned by a Tree!

2. The "Tree" in the Book of Acts

It is of great significance that the Book of Acts, when speaking of the death of Jesus, our Redeeemer, always speaks of Jesus hanging on a TREE!

A number of translations - because people do not understand what a "Tree" is (?), change the word "Tree" and replace it with the word "Cross." The word "Tree" is used in KJV, NKJV and NIV. The word "Cross" is used in LB, Modern Language, Amplified, NAS, Today's Good News, Phillips and NLT.

There is nothing wrong with the word "Cross." It is used much in the Gospels and the Epistles. However, in changing the word "Tree" to the word "Cross", the translators have robbed us of a great truth as seen in the use of the word "Tree!"

In Strong's Concordance, SC.3586, it speaks of "Timber", which by implication is "a stick, club or other wooden article or substance. It is translated as "staff, stocks, tree or wood." It is just a mere word, but the use of the word **TREE** is of great significance in the light of our theme.

- Peter speaks of the death of Jesus "whom they slew and hanged on a TREE" (Acts 4:30).
- Peter speaking again speaks of the death of Jesus, "whom they slew and hanged on a TREE" (Acts 10:39)
- Paul also in speaking of the Lord's death says, "They took Him down from the TREE" (Acts 13:29).

3. The "Tree" in the Book of Galatians

Paul, once again, in speaking of the death of Jesus writes: "Cursed is everyone who hangs on a Tree" (Gal.3:13).

Paul is quoting from the Old Testament which speaks of anyone who hangs on a Tree. The Law said that the body must be taken down from the Tree by sun-down (Deut.21:22,23).

Other examples may be seen in Gen.40:19; Josh.8:29; Esther 2:23.

20

Jesus' body was "hung on a Tree" and was buried before sun-down.

How remarkable that the curse entered mankind and this earth by man partaking of the forbidden Tree and Jesus became a curse for us by hanging on a Tree, the Tree of Calvary!

Thorns and thistles came as a result of God's curse on the earth and Jesus was crowned with thorns and thus became a curse for us on the Tree. It means "impaled on a pale, or, hung on a Tree." It is not until we get to the final chapters of the Book of Revelation (Rev.21-22) that the announcement comes, "And there shall be no more curse." And this is in connection with the Tree of Eternal Life (Rev.22:14; 21:1-6).

4. **The "Tree" in the Epistle of Peter**

Peter, in writing to the believers in his Epistle says that Jesus "who in His own self bore our sins in His body on the Tree" (1Pet.2:24).

When we put these references together, we discover these truths:

- Jesus died on a Tree
- Jesus was hung on the Tree
- Jesus became accursed on the Tree
- He bore our sins in His body on the Tree.
- This was Calvary's Tree. The puzzle comes together. Adam and his wife partook of the forbidden Tree. The curse came on the earth by reason of this Tree. We all bear in our bodies of flesh the Law of sin because of this Tree. Death came by the Tree.

Jesus Himself said: " I am the way, the truth and the life. No man comes to the Father but by Me" (Jhn.14:6).

21

We lost these three in Adam.
- We lost the WAY to the Father
- We lost the TRUTH about the father
- We lost the LIFE of the father,

We lost the way, the truth and the life.

We lost the way to Paradise. We lost the truth when Adam and his wife believed Satan's lie. We lost the Tree of Eternal Life in Adam.

We are driven from the garden of Eden's Paradise.

All that we lost "in Adam" (1Cor.15:22), is restored "in Christ."

Jesus is THE WAY, THE TRUTH and THE LIFE. He is the one and only way to the Father and no one can come to the Father except through Him, our Redeemer, our Restorer and our Lord Jesus Christ.

5. The "Tree" in the Book of Exodus

Hidden away in the Book of Exodus is an amazing short account in the first of Israel's experiences after the exodus from years of slavery to the Egyptians. It is found in Ex.15:22-23. It is a well-worth reading in order to see the relative following points drawn from the passage. The details are noted in brief, while the New Testament shows it's fulfilment in Christ and the Church. There is the counter-part and fulfilment in the Gospels.

Here is the Divine pattern, the parts of the puzzle laid out.
- The 3 days journey- vs.22
- The bitter waters of Marah - vs.23
- The cry to the Lord - vs.24
- The Lord showed Moses A TREE - vs.25

We may ask, Why "a Tree?" The answer: For all the reasons our theme has been about.

- The TREE cast into the bitter waters - vs.25
- The result: the bitter waters are healed
- The Covenant of healing is made with Israel - vs.26
- The Redemptive name is given - "Jehovah Rapha, The Lord who heals - vs.26
- After the 3 days journey, the healing of the bitter waters, the revelation of THE TREE and the healing Covenant of God's redemption, Israel as a nation came to:
  - The 12 wells of water at Elim - vs.27
  - The 70 palm trees - vs.27
  - Thus we have the 3-12-70 pattern seen throughout the Word of God.

Who can fail to see the significance of these intricate details as they unfold in their fulfilment in the New Testament?

- The 3 days and 3 nights of Calvary's experience, the greatest sign given to Jewry - Matt.12:39,40
- The bitter waters in humanity because of the entrance of sin and death
- The cry of need to the Lord
- The revelation of Calvary's TREE cast into the bitter waters of humanity
- The healing of mankind
- The Covenant of healing made with fallen mankind
- The Redemptive name, Jehovah Rapha, fulfilled in the name of the LORD Jesus Christ
- The Twelve apostles sent out to the preach the Gospel of the Kingdom and heal the people - Matt.12
- The Seventy sent out on the same ministry - Lke.10
  - The 3, 12 and 70 pattern in the New Testament.

6. **The "Tree" in the Book of Proverbs**

There are some four references to the Tree of Life in the Book of Proverbs. Each reference may be related back to the beginning as in Genesis.

- Prov.3:18. "Wisdom" is personified in the feminine gender (vs.13-18). In vs.18 it speaks: "She is a Tree of Life to those who take hold of her, and happy are all who retain her." The Tree of the Knowledge of Good and Evil was to make one wise (Gen.3:6) but it was the wrong kind of wisdom (Jas.3:13-18). It was wisdom from below.
- Prov.11:30. "The fruit of the righteous is a Tree of Life, and he who wins souls is wise." Adam and Eve took of the forbidden fruit and became lost souls. In Calvary's Tree we may eat of the right fruit and win souls to Christ at Calvary.
- Prov.13:12. This verse tells us, "Hope deferred makes the heart sick, but when desire comes, it is a Tree of Life. Man, by sin, lost hope and became sick. But through Christ's death, desire is restored and so is the Tree of Eternal Life (Rev.22:14).
- Prov.15:4 tells us: "A wholesome tongue is a Tree of Life, but perverseness in it (the tongue) breaks the spirit." The Serpent came with a forked tongue, deceived Eve with perversity and it broken Adam and Eve's relationship with God, Calvary's Tree only can restore this relationship with the Lord and make the tongue whole again (Note Jas.3:1-12).

7. **The Cross is 'the Tree'**

As already seen, the Cross is A TREE. As we spend time at the Cross and consider the implied truths therein, we discover that there are two sides to that death on Calvary.

24

(i)   There is the death side of this Cross/Tree
(ii)   There is the resurrection side of this Cross/Tree.
        The truth of these two aspects may be seen in the following comments.

- **The Death Side of the Cross**
  The Tree in Eden's Paradise was the Tree of the Knowledge of Good and Evil. Jesus died on Calvary's Tree.
- Sin entered by eating of this forbidden Tree. Sickness and disease came by Adam and his wife eating of this Tree. Jesus took our sickness and disease in His 39 stripes and as He hung on the Tree.
- The curse entered by eating of the Tree of the Knowledge of Good and Evil. Jesus became a curse for us by hanging on a Tree (Gal.3:13; Deut.21:22,23).
- Death entered the human race and passes on to all mankind as the penalty for man's sin of disobedience. "By one man sin entered the world and death by sin..." (Rom.5:11-21). Jesus' death was the penalty on Calvary's Tree. His death was like the first death in Eden, it was substitutionary. He died for us. He died in our stead. "As in Adam all die, even so, in Christ shall all be made alive" (1Cor.15:22). All of Adam's race is born into Satan's Kingdom of Darkness. Jesus died on the Cross/Tree so that we may be born again, born anew, born from above, into the Kingdom of Light and by this act taken out of Satan's Kingdom.
- Thus SIN, SICKNESS, DISEASE, the CURSE and DEATH Jesus suffered for us on the Death-side of the Tree, for all came to Adam's race by a Tree!

- **The Resurrection Side of the Cross**
  On the Resurrection-side of the Cross/Tree, all that mankind lost in Adam is now restored in Christ.
- By man came sin, sickness, disease, the curse and death and the powers of the Kingdom of Darkness. Through Jesus' substitutionary death and His resurrection for us, we can be made righteous, healed and made whole. The curse is lifted and the last enemy to be destroyed is death (1Cor.15),.
- In Adam we also ate of the forbidden Tree. In Christ, and by His resurrection, the Tree of Eternal Life is restored. To him who overcomes and keeps His commandments, which Adam and his wife failed to keep, the Tree of Eternal Life is restored to us. This is clearly seen in the Book of Revelation (Rev.2:1-7; 22:14,19).
- We become a blessing to all the families of the earth and all the nations of the earth (Gen.12:1-4; Gen.22). The blessing of faithful Abraham comes upon us to be a blessing (Gal.3:13,14). We are blessed to bless.
- We are translated out of the Kingdom of Darkness into the Kingdom of Light.
- We were "IN Adam" but now we are "IN Christ." In Adam we partook of the forbidden Tree. In Christ we partake of the Tree of Life, Eternal Life. Refer to the many promises of "eternal life" in John's Gospel. This is the Resurrection-side of the Tree and all the benefits are now available to us in Him!

8. **Back to Faith and Obedience**
   Adam and Eve fell from the ground of faith and obedience to the ground of unbelief and disobedience. Andrew Murray teaches us, "**that Christ died to bring us back to the ground of faith and obedience from which Adam fell.**"

This is why the New Testament (as also the Old) has such a strong emphasis on FAITH and OBEDIENCE! The root sin of Adam and Eve was UNBELIEF internally and then the act of DISOBEDIENCE externally!

We note some important references to these two words in the following Scriptures:

- **FAITH versus UNBELIEF**
  The two words of "faith" and "obedience" is like a two sided coin. Every coin is one but there are two sides to each coin. In the Bible faith equals obedience and unbelief equals disobedience.
  The same example of unbelief - Heb.4:11. KJV
  The same example of disobedience - Heb.4:11. NKJV
  Faith without works (of obedience) is dead - Jas.2:20
  Heb.11 is the great faith chapter. By faith Abraham obeyed…Heb.11:8. Faith equals obedience.
  The underlying words of "faith" and "obedience" are seen throughout the great faith chapter (vs.17-19, 20, 21, 22, 30). The root sin of Eve was unbelief. She believed the word of the Serpent against the Word of God. Unbelief is the root sin. The Holy Spirit comes to convict the world of SIN "because they believe not on Me" (Jhn.16:8-11). Unbelief is the root sin as evidenced in Eden's Paradise.

- **OBEDIENCE versus DISOBEDIENCE**
  The other side of this one and the same coin is obedience versus disobedience. The external act of disobedience was the evident and outworking of the internal root of unbelief in Eden's Garden. By one man's disobedience all were made sinners; by one Man's obedience can all be made righteous (Rom.5:11-21, vs.19,19 and 1Cor.15:46,47). Here we

27

have the acts of the first Adam and the last Adam: disobedience and obedience.

The issue is obedience that arises out of faith and love to the Lord.
"If you will obey My voice..." - Ex.19:5,6
"Obey My voice, but they obeyed not..." - Jer.7:21-28 (Note "obey" five times)
Saul's false confession. "I have obeyed the voice of the Lord" - 1Sam.15:10-26; note vs.19, 20, 22, 24. To obey is better than sacrifice...stubbornness is as iniquity and idolatry.
" A stubborn and rebellious son who will not obey the voice of his father or his mother ..." - Dt.21:18-21.
"If you be willing and obedient..." - Isa.1:19,20.
"If you love Me, keep (obey) My commandments - Jhn.14:15 and also Rom.1:5; 16:18.

The reader is encouraged to refer to Strong's Concordance on the words "faith" and "obedience" or the opposite of these words.

Faith/Unbelief	Obedience/Disobedience
Faith IN the Word	Obedience TO the Word
Strong's Concordance	Strong's Concordance

In Adam we came off the ground of faith and obedience on to the ground of unbelief and disobedience. In Christ we can come off the ground of unbelief and disobedience by coming to Calvary's Tree. It is back to the Word, back to faith and back to obedience. Which ground are we standing on? Which Tree are we feeding on? That is the real issue! This is the Gospel of our Lord Jesus Christ.

28

Summary - The Two Trees

As we bring this Chapter Two to a close, "The Tree of Calvary", we bring the relative points together with the Cross/Tree being central.

It evidences the two sides of Calvary: the Death-side and the Resurrection-side of the Cross, or Tree.

Tree of Good and Evil	Tree of Life
1. Tree of the Knowledge of Good & Evil	1. Tree of Eternal Life restored by redemption
2. Tree forbidden to eat fruit thereof	2. Mankind invited to eat & live - Jhn.6:53,54
3. Death comes by eating	3. Life comes by eating - 1Cor.11
4. Sin, disease on the unborn race	4. Righteousness, healing & health available
5. Curse & thorns come by this Tree	5. Jesus crowned with thorns, & accursed
6. In the Garden of Eden	6. In a Garden - Jhn.19:11
7. Tree in the Midst - Gen.2:9	7. In the midst - Jhn.19:18
8. Two thieves - Adam and Eve	8. Two thieves - Matt.27:38
9. By one man's disobedience	9. By one Man's obedience - Rom.5:11-21
10. Cast out of earthly Paradise	10. Paradise & Tree of Life open in heaven - Lke.23:39-43; Rev.2:7

29

CHAPTER THREE

THE TREE OF ETERNAL LIFE

In this Chapter we finish our "Tale of Three Trees."

1. **The Tree of Life in the Book of Revelation**
   The Bible opens in Genesis with two Trees: the Tree of the Knowledge of Good and Evil and the Tree of Eternal Life. The emphasis in Genesis is upon the forbidden Tree, with the death penalty attached upon disobedience.

   We can safely assume (not presume) that the other Tree - not forbidden - was the Tree of Eternal Life. This is seen in Genesis because when God drove the man and the woman out of the Garden, He said, "Man is become one of US and now lest he take of the tree of life, and eat, and live forever, He drove out the man and the woman. He also placed the Cherubim and the flaming sword to keep and guard the way to this Tree of Life. The reason: If man had eaten of the Tree of Eternal Life they would have lived for ever in an unredeemable state, so God drove the man and his wife out of the earthly Paradise.

   In the Gospels, Acts and the Epistles, we see the Tree of Calvary, both the death and the resurrection sides, as commented on in the previous chapter.

   But in the Book of Revelation, we see but one Tree, the Tree of Eternal Life. All is restored in the final Book of the Bible. Adam and Eve partook of the forbidden Tree. Man forfeited the Tree of Eternal Life. Jesus came and died on Calvary's Tree to restore to us the Tree of Eternal Life. This is why there is but the one Tree seen in the Book of Revelation.

It may be asked: Why is one Tree mentioned in Revelation? What about the Tree of the Knowledge of Good and Evil? The sad reason undoubtedly is that the this Tree has exhausted its fruitfulness in the tragic history of the human race. Mankind has been feeding on the fruit of that Tree for some 6000 years. Man knows good and evil. History has seen the best and the worst, the good and the evil fruit of that Tree in human history.

Because of Christ's sacrifice on the Tree of Calvary, an end is made of sin and time has made an end of that Tree. Jesus died on Calvary's Tree to restore to us the Tree of Eternal Life.

We note the relevant verses in Revelation on the restoration through redemption of the Tree of Eternal Life.

- **Rev.2:1-7**
Ephesus was the first of the Churches to receive a letter from the Lord, via the apostle John. It was the FIRST Church that had left its FIRST love. It was called to REPENT, the FIRST word of the Gospel (Mrk.1:15) and to do the FIRST works.
The FIRST promise given to the overcomers by hearing the Spirit was: "To him who overcomes, I will give to eat from the Tree of Life, which is in the midst of the Paradise of God" (vs.7). Man lost the earthly Paradise of God and the Tree of Eternal Life, and now, through Jesus, the heavenly Paradise of God

31

is opened again and the Tree of Eternal Life is restored.

- **Rev.22:1-6**

  In the vision here, John sees the new and heavenly Jerusalem and a new heaven and new earth. He sees a river of the water of life proceeding from the throne of God and the Lamb. As he sees the river of God, he also sees the Trees of Life, which bore twelve manner of fruit for each month of the year. There was no more curse and all in that city would see the face of God and His name (His nature) would be in their foreheads. What a contrast to that which came on mankind in Genesis.

- **Rev.22:14,19**

  "Blessed are those who do His commandments (or wash their robes), that they may have the right to the Tree of Life and may enter through the gates of the city."

  In vs.19, "...God shall take away his part from the Book of Life (Margin. Tree of Life. NLT), from the holy city, and from the things which are written in this book."

  Adam and his bride failed to keep His commandment not to eat of the forbidden Tree and thus forfeited the Tree of Eternal Life.

  Through Calvary's Tree, this Tree is restored to those who will keep His commandments; those who have washed their robes in the blood of the Lamb, our Redeemer and our Saviour.

32

It is the Tree of the Knowledge of Good and Evil in Genesis.

It is the Tree of Calvary in the Gospels.

It is the Tree of Eternal Life in the Revelation. The first thing Adam lost is the first promise given!

2. Making an End of Sin

In Dan.9:24-27 we have the tremendous prophesy of Messiah's ministry on the Cross. He would finish the transgression, made an end of sin and make reconciliation for iniquity. These three - transgression, sin and iniquity, were dealt with on Calvary's Tree, first of all, legally or judicially, and then practically and actually. Genesis completes the picture for us in Revelation.

When Adam and Eve sinned, falling from the ground of faith and obedience, they received a knowledge which they did not have before. It was the Tree of the Knowledge of Good and Evil. It was not just "the Tree of Evil." It was the Tree of the Knowledge of BOTH Good and Evil. It was a dual knowledge, but the inward bend was to do evil.

The moment they sinned, the law of conscience came into operation, "their thoughts the meanwhile accusing or else excusing each other" (Rom.2:14,15).

Though they were created perfect, it would seem that the law of conscience was inactive, as they were in a state of innocence. But the entrance of the knowledge of sin triggered conscience into effect. This is evident by so many things, a few of which we list out here.

33

- They knew they had violated God's law-word. They had disobeyed His one commandment, His one "you shall not...."
- They became fearful and afraid and hid themselves from the voice of His presence
- They knew that they were naked and sought to cover their shame by the fig-leaves. Even today, man is clothed with a covering, and generally speaking, no one goes about naked
- They had their "guilt and blame game" on God, each other and then the Serpent, rather than each own their sinful condition
- They knew the judgments of God, for sin must be judged by a holy and righteous God.

Paul, in the Epistle to the Romans, follows some of the Genesis procedures, as seen in the following:

(i)   By one man's disobedience many were made (constituted) sinners (as already noted). Read Rom.5:11-21 with 1Cor.15:21,22. By one man sin entered the world, and death by sin. In Adam all sinned, We fell when Adam fell, as we were yet in his loins, as yet unborn. We all come under Adam's condemnation.

(ii)   In Rom.6, the "old man" is Adam, the first man, and from Adam we have received "the body of sin." Outside of Christ, we used the members of our body as servants of sin. Now in Christ, we are to reckon ourselves dead to sin, and use these members as servants to God.

(iii)   Rom.7 may be referred to as "the Tree of the Knowledge of Good and Evil." Why?

- The personal pronouns (KJV. "I", "me" and "my") are used some 36 times in this chapter.
- The words "good and evil" (KJV) are used some six times and two times respectively. These verses are worthy of note, especially the major verse. Paul speaks of his own struggle over this internal Tree.
- "For I know that in me (that is, my flesh) dwells no **GOOD** thing: for to will is present with me; but how to perform that which is **GOOD**, I find not.

  For the **GOOD** that I would I do not; but the **EVIL** which I would not, that I do. Now if I do that which I would not, it is no more I that do it, but **SIN** dwells in me.

  I find then a **LAW** (we could say, A **TREE**), that, when I would do **GOOD**, **EVIL** is present with me" (Rom.7:18-21).

All of this language belongs to the Tree of the Knowledge of Good and Evil. When he wants to do good, evil is present with him. And this is true of all believers. Why? Because we partook of the Tree of Good and Evil "in Adam."

There is the "seed-sin" in the "fruit" and the "fruit" was in the Tree (Gen.1:11,12). It was in the forbidden fruit. This is the law of sin in this body of death (Rom.7:22-25). Deliverance is only through Christ from this "law of sin."

(iv)   Rom.8 may be called "the Tree of Eternal Life". The key word in this chapter refers to "life" some five times. It also speaks of the Holy Spirit or the Spirit, or the Spirit of Life some 21 times.
"For the law of the Spirit of LIFE IN Christ Jesus has made me free from the law of sin and death" (Rom.8:2).

It may come as a shock to many believers that Rom.8:2 is true in spirit but not so physically. The verse needs to be read carefully, prayerfully, thoughtfully and intelligently.

The verse tells us that the law of the Spirit of life in Christ Jesus has made us FREE from the law of SIN and DEATH! If this is physically true, then why do believers sin and why do believers die physically?

When we come to God, through Christ, all our sins are forgiven, BUT the law of sin, or the sin nature, is not yet eradicated. That law of sin (or the Tree of the Knowledge of Good and Evil) is still in us.

This is where the believer's battle is. This is where spiritual warfare is fought. Peter tells us to "abstain from fleshly lusts that WAR against the soul" (1Pet.2:11). And Paul tells us in his writings that, we are to crucify the affections and lust, reckoning ourselves to be dead unto sin (Rom.6:6; Gal.5:24).

John also remind us that "...IF we sin, we have an advocate with the Father, Jesus Christ" (Read carefully 1Jhn.1:6--2:4 noting the seven "if's" in these verses. KJV).

36

In Conclusion:
If we use the illustration of being on an aircraft, there are two laws in operation. These are (a) The law of gravity - what goes up must come down - and (b) the law of aero-dynamics.

As long as the plane is fuelled continually, it can fly in this higher law of aero-dynamics. It is "free" from the law of gravity. However, the pilot must also realize that, though the plane is "free" from the law of gravity, that law is not eradicated.

In application, "the Law of the Spirit" makes the believer "free" from "the Law of sin and death" BUT that law is not yet eradicated from our being. As long as the believer lives in this HIGHER LAW of the Spirit of Life in Christ Jesus, he is "free" from the law of sin and death. However, this law is not yet eradicated. The sin nature is not eradicated! We are not yet sinless beings. We are not yet sinlessly perfect.

The believer must also realize that, unless they are alive to the coming of the Lord (1Thess.4:15-18), and the rapture of the Church with the resurrected saints to meet the Lord in air and be for ever with Him, all will keep their final appointment with death (Heb.9:27).
The last thing to be redeemed is our body (Eph.1:14; 4:30).
The last enemy to be destroyed is death (1Cor.15:25,26). When we receive our incorruptible and glorified bodies, then Rom.8:2 will be fully and physically realized.

37

In the meantime, let us "live and walk in the Spirit" (the higher law), and "war a good warfare" against the world, the flesh and the Devil, realizing that the law of sin and death is not yet eradicated (the lower law).This lower law is the law of spiritual gravity.

Who can really and truly and honestly say that they are physically free from the law of sin and death, or sinlessly perfect? It is this truth that keeps us walking in the light and in humility of mind before the Lord unto "that perfect day" (Prov.4:18,19).

The truth of these things will save any believer from becoming a grace-abuser. We will not live in sin that grace may abound, though we have great appreciation for the grace of God in our lives (Jude 3,4; Rom.5:21; 6:1,2;1Pet.5:12).

In Revelation, there is no more sin, curse or death. All has been dealt with at the Cross, the Tree of Calvary. Life is restored. Paradise is opened for those who keep His commandments.

The full manifestation of Messiah's ministry is evidenced, made possible by Calvary's Tree. There is an end of transgression, an end made of sin, and complete reconciliation for iniquity is manifested. What was possible is now actualized; what was idealistic is now realistic.

It's your choice!

In Deut.30:15-20 we find these words:

"Behold! I have set before you today life and good, and death and evil,
in that I command you today to love Jehovah your God, to walk in His ways, and to keep His commandments and His statutes and His judgments, so that you may live and multiply. And Jehovah your God shall bless you in the land where you go to possess it.
But if you turn away your heart, so that you will not hear, but shall be drawn away and worship other gods and serve them,
I declare to you today that you shall surely perish; you shall not prolong *your* days on the land where you pass over Jordan to go to possess it.
I call Heaven and earth to record today against you. I have set before you life and death, blessing and cursing. Therefore, choose life, so that both you and your seed may live,
so that you may love Jehovah your God, *and* that you may obey His voice, and that you may cling to Him. For He is your life and the length of your days, so that you may dwell in the land which Jehovah swore to your fathers, to Abraham, to Isaac, and to Jacob, to give it to them."

It is most fitting that, what God spoke to the new generation of Israel, through Moses, is that with which we conclude our "Tale of Three Trees."

Verses 15 and 19 is just another way of the Lord setting before Israel, as He did before Adam and eve, these two Trees, as in the Book of Genesis.

"See, I have set before you today
- Life and good
- Death and evil.
I call heaven and earth as witnesses today against you, that I have set before
- Life and death
- Blessing and cursing
- Therefore CHOOSE LIFE
- That both you and your seed may LIVE
- That you may LOVE the Lord your God
- That you may OBEY His voice
- And that you may CLING to Him
- For HE is your life
- And the length of your days..."

In other words, the Lord says: "I have set before you today TWO TREES, the Tree of the Knowledge of Good and Evil and the Tree of Eternal Life...therefore choose the Tree of Eternal Life, that you and your seed may live, love, obey and live on the earth."

It is your choice!

AMEN and AMEN!

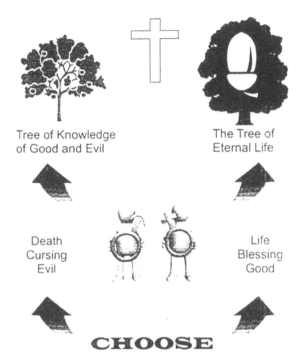

Tree of Knowledge of Good and Evil

The Tree of Eternal Life

Death
Cursing
Evil

Life
Blessing
Good

CHOOSE

Ground of
Unbelief

Ground of
Faith

DISOBEDIENCE

OBEDIENCE

The Law-Word-Will of God

1. _____
2. _____
3. _____
4. _____
5. _____
6. _____
7. _____

Bibliography

1. Arthur W. Pink - "Gleanings in Genesis." Moody Press, USA -1950. Ch.2. Pages 27-32
2. Notes - Watchman Nee (Tract)
3. Interpreting the Scriptures - K. J. Conner & K .P. Malmin - Australian Edition -1976
4. King James Bible - Public Domain
5. New King James Bible - Nelson Publishers

Capitalization on 'Tree' throughout booklet - the writer - Kevin J. Conner

About the Author

Born in Melbourne, Australia in 1927 and saved at the age of 14, Kevin Conner served the Lord in the Salvation Army until the age of 21. At this time he entered pastoral ministry for several years. After that, he was involved in teaching ministry in Australia, New Zealand and for many years at Bible Temple in Portland, Oregon. After serving as Senior Minister of Waverley Christian Fellowship for eight years (1987-1994), he continued to serve the church locally as well as ministering at various conferences and the continued writing of textbooks.

Kevin is recognised internationally as a teaching-apostle after his many years in both church and Bible College ministry. His textbooks have been used by ministers and students throughout the world. He has been in great demand as a teacher and has travelled extensively. Kevin passed away peacefully in Melbourne, Australia in February 2019 at the age of 92.

Visit Kevin's web site at www.kevinconner.org for more details about his life and ministry, as well as information about his 75+ books, his video courses, and his audio teaching podcast.

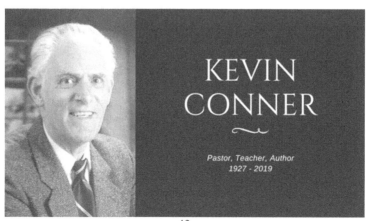

KEVIN
CONNER

Pastor, Teacher, Author
1927 - 2019

Kevin's Autobiography

Kevin Conner is known by many people around the world as a theologian, Bible teacher, and best-selling author of over 75 biblical textbooks. Although thousands of people have been impacted by his ministry and his writings, only a few people know his personal story. Kevin took the time to detail his own life journey, including lessons gleaned along the way, in his auto-biography "This is My Story" back in 2007. It is now available in the following formats:

- PDF download - visit www.kevinconner.org/shop
- International paperback or eBook from Amazon.
- Australian paperback from WORD books (www.word.com.au).

Kevin was an orphan who never met his dad or mum. He grew up in boy's homes before coming to faith in Jesus Christ in the Salvation Army in his teenage years. From there, his life took many turns as he continued to pursue his faith in God and his understanding of the Scriptures and church life. Follow his journey and gain wisdom for your own life and ministry as you read his intriguing life-story.

Other Books by Kevin Conner

Acts, A Commentary
An Evaluation of Joseph Prince's Book 'Destined to Reign'
Are Women Elders Biblical?
Biblical Principles of Leadership
The Christian Millennium
1 & 2 Chronicles, a Commentary
1 Corinthians, a Commentary
The Church in the New Testament
The Church of the Firstborn and the Birthright
1 & 2 Chronicles, A Commentary
Colossians and Philemon, A Commentary
The Covenants (with Ken Malmin)
Daily Devotions (or Ministrations)
Daniel, An Exposition
The Day After the Sabbath
The Death-Resurrection Route
Deuteronomy, A Commentary
Esther, A Commentary
Exodus, A Commentary
Ezekiel, A Commentary
The Feasts of Israel
First Principles of the Doctrine of Christ
Foundations of Christian Doctrine
Foundations of Christian Doctrine (Self Study Guide)
Foundational Principles of Church Membership
Foundation Principles of the Doctrine of Christ
Frequently Asked Questions
Galatians, A Commentary
Genesis, A Commentary
Headship, Covering and Hats

Hebrews, A Commentary
The House of God
Interpreting the Book of Revelation
Interpreting the Scriptures (with Ken Malmin)
Interpreting the Scriptures (Self Study Guide)
Interpreting the Symbols and Types
Isaiah, A Commentary
James, A Commentary
Jeremiah and Lamentations, A Commentary
Joshua, A Commentary
Jude, A Commentary
Judges, A Commentary
Keep Yourself Pure
The Kingdom Cult of Self
Kings of the Kingdom - Character Studies on Israel's Kings
Law and Grace
Leviticus, A Commentary
The Lord Jesus Christ our Melchizedek Priest
Maintaining the Presence
Marriage, Divorce and Remarriage
Messages from Matthew
Methods and Principles of Bible Research
Ministries in the Cluster
The Ministry of Women
The Minor Prophets, A Commentary Mystery
Mystery Parables of the Kingdom
The Name of God
New Covenant Realities
New Testament Survey (with Ken Malmin)
Numbers, A Commentary
Old Testament Survey (with Ken Malmin)

Only for Catholics
Passion Week Chart
Philippians, A Commentary
Psalms, A Commentary
The Relevance of the Old Testament to a New Testament
Church Restoration Theology
Restoration Theology
Revelation, A Commentary
Romans, A Commentary
The Royal Seed
Ruth, A Commentary
1 & 2 Samuel, A Commentary
Sermon Outlines (3 volumes)
The Seventy Weeks Prophecy
Studies in the Royal Priesthood
The Sword and Consequences
The Tabernacle of David
The Tabernacle of Moses
The Temple of Solomon
Table Talks
Tale of Three Trees
1 & 2 Thessalonians, A Commentary
This is My Story (Kevin Conner's autobiography)
This We Believe
Three Days and Three Nights (with Chart)
Tithes and Offerings
Today's Prophets
To Drink or Not to Drink
To Smoke or Not to Smoke
Two Kings and a Prince
Understanding the New Birth and the Baptism of the Holy
Spirit

Vision of an Antioch Church
Water Baptism Thesis
What About Israel?

Visit www.kevinconner.org for more information.
Visit www.amazon.com/author/kevinjconner for a list of other books by Kevin Conner.

Video Training Seminars

Kevin Conner's popular "Key of Knowledge" Seminar is now available as an online teaching course. Part 1 covers 'Methods and Principles of Bible Research' and includes over 6 hours of video teaching, the required textbooks, extra hand out notes, and a self-guided online study program. The first lesson, 'Challenge to Study' is FREE.

The second part of Kevin Conner's "Key of Knowledge" Seminar is about 'Interpreting the Bible' and includes over 7 hours of video teaching, two downloadable textbooks, extra hand out notes, and a self-guided online study program. These two courses can be taken as stand-alone courses, in succession, or simultaneously.

Also available at www.kevinconner.org/courses is Kevin's extensive teaching on his best-selling book The Foundation of Christian Doctrine, which includes 67 videos which can be purchased in 4 parts.

Visit the courses page at www.kevinconner.org for all the details.

Kevin Conner's Audio Teaching

Dozens of Kevin Conner's messages are available on his FREE teaching podcast - 'Kevin Conner Teaches'. This podcast is accessible from Apple Podcasts, Google Podcasts, or Spotify Podcasts (if you are a subscriber), as well as at www.kevinconner.podbean.com (including on the Podbean mobile App).

New messages are published weekly, selected from messages Kevin has given over the years at various churches, conferences, and training seminars. Be sure to subscribe so you are notified of recent releases.

Visit https://www.kevinconner.org/audios-by-kevin/ for a full list of podcast titles and series.

PDF Versions of Kevin Conner's Books

All of Kevin Conner's books are now available to purchase in quality PDF format. This digital format is in addition to the Kindle eBooks and paperback/hardback versions currently available. A PDF is a 'portable document format' used on all computers for reading documents. Books in this format can be read on a computer, laptop, or handheld device and/or printed out for your personal use (even stored in your own binding of choice). Many PDF readers also allow you to 'mark-up' and add your own notes to the document. PDFs of Kevin's books are for your personal use and are not for copying or redistribution.

You can purchase PDF books at www.kevinconner.org/shop. Upon payment, a download link will be sent to you via email along with your receipt.

Resources by Mark Conner

Kevin Conner's son, Mark Conner, worked closely with him in the church ministry for many years (as music director and youth pastor), before succeeding him in 1995 as the Senior Minister of what was then Waverley Christian Fellowship (now CityLife Church) Mark transitioned out of that role in early 2017 and since that time has been giving himself to speaking, training, coaching, and writing.

Here is a list of Mark's books which may be of interest to you:

* *Transforming Your Church - Seven Strategic Shifts*
* *Money Talks: Practical Wisdom for Becoming Financially Free*
* *The Spiritual Journey: Understanding the Stages of Faith*
* *How to Avoid Burnout: Five Habits of Healthy Living*
* *Prison Break: Finding Personal Freedom*
* *Pass the Baton: Successful Leadership Transition*
* *Successful Christian Ministry*

These can be purchased from:
* Amazon.com/author/markconner in paperback and eBook format.
* WORD books in Australia (www.word.com.au)
* www.kevinconner.org/books-by-mark-conner/ in PDF format.

Mark also has an active BLOG and teaching podcast. Visit www.markconner.com.au for more information.

Made in United States
Cleveland, OH
12 February 2025

14313010R00036